Praise for
## UNEARTH [THE FLOWERS]

"Gratitude to Thea for finding life amongst what is so often stepped on underestimated and misnamed. Honor to Thea for listening to the loudness in the small. Praise to Thea for the magnitude of this healing which is big enough for all of us."
— ALEXIS PAULINE GUMBS, author of *Spill: Scenes of Black Feminist Fugitivity*

"Pick up this book, and read. *Unearth [The Flowers]* reveals the language of resilience, resistance, and power, and each poem demonstrates that we cultivate our own healing."
— E. K. KEITH, author of *Ordinary Villains*

"*Unearth [The Flowers]* sees the pastoral tradition of poetry through a contemporary feminist lens that shows Thea Matthews as a writer of urgency and authentic concern. Or as Matthews herself says, 'where there is land / there is blood.' This is a book of catalogue, of taxonomy, of the need to name the earth and stand on it whole."
— JERICHO BROWN, author of *The Tradition*

"Thea Matthews's *Unearth [The Flowers]* is an exquisite debut poetry collection. Ultimately, it is universal in its breadth, rich in imagery, heartbreaking in its scope, and affirming in its ability to center resiliency of the human spirit."
— JP HOWARD, author of *SAY/MIRROR*

"Thea Matthews is a poetic herbalist, using flowers to create healing. This work is egalitarian, touching on blooms of all sorts: indigenous, imported, bolted, and cultivated. You will feel these poems in the root of your jaw, in your foot arches. Matthews is an experienced poet with a deft hand and an honest heart. These words languidly stretch, snap like a lock blade, they drape and twine and reach. Read this work and be changed."
— KIM SHUCK, San Francisco Poet Laureate

D1545989

"Thea Matthews's poems excavate and explore family traumas and relationships. Voice and silence deliver deep beauty and urgency. This is a language of flesh, blood, soil, sorrow, and ultimately healing. Matthews's *Unearth [The Flowers]* is a bold and remarkable debut poetry collection."

— MAW SHEIN WIN, author of *Invisible Gifts: Poems*

"*Unearth [The Flowers]* is a blooming battle cry, a feat of alchemy in which the personal and political merge in a brutal empathy. Rage and sorrow and the liberation of healing unfurl in a landscape of flowers—this is true literary witchcraft."

— MICHELLE TEA, author of *Against Memoir*

"Matthews's careful investigation of each flower paired with an emotional journey is ambitious poetic work which deserves careful attention—these poems are crucial for our times."

— MK CHAVEZ, author of *Mothermorphosis* and *Dear Animal,*

"When the wickedness and perfidiousness of humans and the vagaries and cruelties of fate create their wreckage in us, it seems prudent to describe the results in terms of the delicacies of flowers. This is what Thea Matthews has done in this, her intelligent and magnificent debut collection."

— NATASHA DENNERSTEIN, author of *Seahorse* and coauthor of *Turn and Face the Strange*

"*Unearth [The Flowers]* is a refusal of silence and a testament to survival, speaking back to the damages with a gorgeous bouquet of poems. Thea Matthews conjures poetic magic for healing and bearing witness with vibrant, lyrically rich poems."

— TIANA CLARK, author of *I Can't Talk About the Trees Without the Blood*

"Thea Matthews is the voice and protector of our generation. Brave poems like a universe that has decided to go forward with a third testament. Thea Matthews is our sacred underground; the only host of our ascension."

— TONGO EISEN-MARTIN, author of *Heaven Is All Goodbyes*

# UNEARTH [THE FLOWERS]

# UNEARTH
## [THE FLOWERS]

## THEA MATTHEWS

RED LIGHT
lit

Red Light Lit Press
www.redlightlit.com
San Francisco, California

ISBN 13: 978-0-9998895-1-0
Library of Congress Control Number: 2019957980
First edition, printed February 2020

Publisher: Jennifer Lewis
Editor: Jessie Carver
Illustration: elle hell, @ellehell
Book design & layout: Jessie Carver
Text set in Neutraface Text & Adobe Garamond Pro

Printed in the United States of America

Made with love

*for Barbara*

I know flowers shine stronger
than the sun
their eclipse means the end of
times

—ETEL ADNAN

# Contents

PRELUDE | *Praeludium*


UNEARTH   the abuse : repetition of bruising the spirit
the silence two o'clock in the morning
the mother in silence
the memories of a child
the child / mother     stolen
the generations like weeds ossified
the apathy of those already dead with a pulse
the time said once more
                 *ssshhhh . . . don't tell no body*


the refusal to believe me when I tried to speak
the suffering of seeking vengeance
the vengeance to kill
the rage inflaming my body
the truth on my lips
the screams in the back of my throat
the cries trapped in my teeth
the tongue clipped        now regrown


UNEARTH   [THE FLOWERS]

# PERENNIAL

## INDIGO | *Baptisia australis*


Open :: I baptize you

in the wild blue gold      the pliable weed-like
flowers      your body     saturated
in the granules    of lapis lazuli
sprouts from      tears copulating with cash crops
the edible gold and blue denim
armies of unknown rebels      too black to
ever be burned at the stake   gambol in
the rings of your eyes.
                    You   my beloved   are to be cherished
Your curls   are yours not for porcelain heads      or
zookeeper fingers
Your skin    cannot be worn by sunspots
and soft credit cards
Your lips    are the softest chewable rims
sucking the seeds of terra cotta sunsets
and your feet follow the rhythm      earth
will move    to rip      the renewal from urban

on red soil.

## CLEMATIS | *Clematis virginiana*


you found me
at the bottom of the Pacific

quiet and still
whales preserved my amethyst light

to glow in
the dark despite    floating dreams    I failed

to live    I
jumped to live    I know why smiles stroll

I was told
ribcages break    when grasping their last breath

deflated
from collapsed lungs    overwhelmed with grief

I stopped    here

## SEASIDE DAISY | *Erigeron glaucus*


not everyone     swims the depth I swim
faces appear disappear then reappear on oil
stained streets    and for once I would like to go a week
without thinking of him     his death haunts me
like a relentless weed   who grows all-year-round
occupies the soil in a sit-in    defies time
protests the seasons    calls my name to the shore
I once called body    waves wash over me    I am home
eyes navigable    body a blimp    blood purified
waves dissolve memories : the names we print on sand
I swore his fingers would grow old with the silver
strands of his hair but they will not

he left before me

BLEEDING HEART | *Lamprocapnos spectabilis*


I felt my last heart beat
took my last full breath
closed my eyes the moment
old hands touched my body

and my blood screamed
desperate to rinse blood
as much as skin   my kin
I found the ocean's floor

I live in the streaming
tears of new bedrock     now
old hands cannot harm me

no more.

EVENING PRIMROSE | *Oenothera biennis*


The sun probes into my leaves
  stops the hurt
      breaks my heart
          o        p      e      n
Opposition
stands with harmony

Extreme polarities
are first found in the mind

No one is born guilty

Mine flutter within
so close my petals crinkle

I burst
      one by one
      inconstantly
      wildly
trembling vowels clasping consonance

Shaming another
for the instinct to inflict pain when hurt
keeps no one accountable

To heal is the antonym of hurt

Each twilight you hear me
unfold      reveal myself
to the rising moon
I never apologize for crying

I just cry      I breathe what
can never be privatized
No one   will ever own

the contracts muscles have
the release of tension they sign

I      am Evening Primrose
I take responsibility for all that is mine

and let you claim yours

CAROLINA LUPINE | *Thermopsis villosa*


frizzy black curls       twist and swirl
a wide halo
from tangled knots       in the South


we rise       within a golden
spiral   on green
malachite stems   tapering


off at the tips       with enough
heat       and pressure
stubborn mountains       become   scarred


valleys       thin tributaries
to clandestine
basins     veins meander like


railroad tracks built by torn hands
land reminds us
your ancestors conjured you


believe them       through their howling
laments   keloid
backs       blood-stained rags   they slept


lived     ate and picked       cash crops in
burnt sienna
rooted in       plantations built


on red soil   skin smooth of

Lupine     we shine
near sprouted wolves in meadows


we rise in weaves of blue blood
warrior          oppressed
colonizer                    colonized


in one          when we cry I see
even when tumid
eyes clamp shut     when seething with


the tears   I scream   cry   growl
shake my body
dangle my arms     sway my hips


raise my left fist   trudge the road
purify blood
through spirit      I remember


the remedy of my own
body and soul
is within me and through you

## CROCUS | *Crocus sativus*


Amethyst Crocus
a voice once voiceless
I speak with several
tongues at once. The first
to arrive in spring—
I unroll my tongue
refuse silence break
silence. No man can
ever tell me *sssshhhh*         again!
I loosen the drapes
rise    levitate    glide
in the air of a
cerulean sky
where   helicopters
and drones swarm over
my head.    Lakota
elders remind me :
everyone must be
protected         despite
color   class   creed.    Water
cannons try to break
prayers.    I duck from
tear gas          and rubber
bullets.   Together
we end cycles of
abuse.    We wave flares
over bridges a-
cross intersections
throughout   long   marches
proclaiming : our lives
our bodies    our health    matters!
With     pen to paper
petals of my pride
die        I turn inward.

IRIS | *Iris germanica*


I.


The color of my eyes    the ring of dilation
transmits the screams      coughed blood
of those who died in resistance    those who strangled
with rosaries and hid
behind crucifixes           those possessed by rambling
spirits         in the early
hours of the Sabbath    and then  those who remain
stuck       between dirt and dry-
ing pavement.    In the summer     my eyes unearth lies
once told    force-fed to be
made true       for the mother and father inside me
to the children passing
by     to the adults aimlessly walking on my
tongue.     I sing spirituals : hymns for our freedom.
Rooted from a thin stem
I elongate my neck    bridging the gap between
heaven and earth    the path
between me and my kin.    Generations of eyes
closed      meet those  wide  o   p   e   n
tongues flail    knees to an unsound   national anthem.

II.

My eyes gaze
at children
conditioned
to play dead
provide sex-
ual favors
to preachers
           politicians
                       teachers
in a land
where     life is
reduced to
a brand : a
marketing
campaign : re-
ality
TV    where
the cool    are
conditioned
to crave fame
want nothing
more    than to
die rich     these
children will
starve over-
weight        others
will die in
denial
more will die
next to stran-
gers respons-
ible      for
excavat-
ing    little
organs

GARDENIA | *Gardenia jasminoides*


Breathe

A call    to    learn
                 love
                 listen     to that if you need to
                 speak

Speak
rather than resist
refine your lungs      purify
the blood circulating the sun
inhale the scent of my evergreen

Exhale
my forgiveness
of dead trees the
pollen found only in summer

Feel
the continuous chant
the marching in your veins
The army lives within you

ORCHID | *Phalaenopsis*


Fluttery opalescent moth wings
orbit my light.
Strong North Dakota winds
remind me— stay humbled.
Jolted awake (silence)
           the stillness of joy
                   absence of incarnation
                           cessation of all desires
               await remembrance.
Although my eyes saw the first sunrise
my heart remembers the harvest.
Seeds    root themselves in fecund soil
        seeds grow          in solitude.
Orchids          equanimous and upright
unfold their fuchsia arms with a subtle grin. They
hum—         strong soul
r     e     b     l     o     o     m.
Never doubt your propensity to
radiate boundless light. When you
see a moth        Spirit is near you.
Stand tall.
Illuminate your decipherment of what is true:


You are worthy of love.


You are more than        locked bedroom doors
                         screaming into pillows
                         signed executive orders
                         confederate lies
                         sputtering "you don't belong here!"

You are more than     crying on cold bathroom tile floors
treacherous red-tie speeches
military missiles      drones
bullets erupting arteries
bombs bulldozing the home.

You are more than     clenched fists
spray-canned "die pigs"
tear gas defiling your lungs
shattered bank windows
masked faces    rifles
black combat boots
splitting faces on asphalt

more than borders     more than skin
Your blood fertilizes this land our land we
give birth to.   You are whole     complete.

Complete like impermeable heat
feel Spirit's long-lasting embrace :
the embryonic rhythm of life     (my god)
you are immortal.     In your mind    serpents
hiss  you are hopeless helpless
nothing more than the incest
believe you are nothing
believe you are powerless
wallowing in an empty riverbed
with a worn noose tied around your neck.
Remember     strong soul
your tears : shackles created by someone else's fears
flood your cavern with inflammable oily water.

Purify!      Keep the lungs and heart untied.
Relax the spine.     Stretch the groin.

Today's march was yesterday's frontline.
Tomorrow is another struggle.

## HIBISCUS | *Hibiscus rosa-sinensis*


I.


legs bruised        found entangled
within the branches of
tropical crimson shrubs
shrouded    by old brick and
mortar    yet      alive
my golden pink pistil
protrudes    dangles in the
hot wind    my eyes yawn a
litany for survival
I struggle to stand      collapsed
three times before grasping
trees with my fingernails
my petals radiate
a vibrancy       still         un-
touched    prepare! I wail    prepare to survive        more than
uncontrollable hands

II.

infiltration
human sex trafficking
counter-intelligence
high surveillance
programs established
by dubious politicians
children nameless
blazing temples
covered-up
assassinations
severed limbs
florescent lights
blood vessels pop
peeled foreskin back

Who this poem is for
may never read this page
yet I am with you
ready
for transcendence

Freedom

Our deliverance
from unspoken unseen
always felt
disdain aggression.
And how micro is it
when every fiber
in your being feels it?
Having to prove
discrimination exists
tells us
the sky isn't blue
unless
we know

precisely
the molecules in the air
scattering the sun's blue light
in spite of the fact
we both witness
the sky is blue without measurement

We need no measurement to confirm hate
We need no measurement to confirm denial
We need no empowerment

Our own power
restores us

No expertise
No diagnoses

Trust your lived experience
Intuition can never fail us

Cleanse the river!

Unearth
faulty roots     flowers dead
watch new seeds grow
feel     Spirit and blood
band a double helix

Your medicine
        your healing
                your recovery
lives within you.

## MAGNOLIA | *Magnolia grandiflora*


Waxed hands forge freedom:
the unshakable knowing the wealth of
life dwells in the breath. No one can
define my value. Pacific winds sing

my name from the palm of my rhythm to
the arteries' cascading waves     my bones
penetrate pavement. Each centennial
bole decimates the lines in parking lots

old street signs near newly bought commercial
space   homes now banned to families
who once lived there. Remembering their names
my pollen becomes prayers. I release

a tantalizing fragrance sleepless beetles
yearn for. My cretaceous fingers unfurl
I gaze at the spirits who trap others   lost spirits
doped up on narcotics   spirits who struggle to

recognize their own light. Only those willing
see through trees     taste my breath
on Sunday afternoons.

NOPAL CACTUS | *Opuntia macrocentra*


as above     so below
as within     so without
the principle  of correspondence     between
my prickly body     cocooning
in the solitude of the desert
and the oceanic waves     eroding the ridge
no one else sees   is


the metamorphosis
of butterflies    suspended
in the smokescreens     of cerulean mountains
in the pale magenta clouds
in the body I call sacred     held up by chastity
under a sky     cursed by a relentless sun
burned in the pores of my blossom


I am the Nopal Cactus
my grandfather would slice me each morning
trim my thorns     cook me with scrambled eggs
eat me with corn tortillas   I
am the Prickly Pear no one else would touch
I thought life was too hard to bare
until     my thorns grew back     until


I held the chalice     until I drank
the water of my mother's womb     until I rose
slowly in the heat     each droplet of prism light
streaming down as tears   I
am the life : the protective force of transformation
In late spring
I bloom only in midmorning


by nightfall   I dance
where no one can touch me
I am safe

CHERRY PLUM | *Prunus cerasifera*


Touch me and I might kill you. I
am a wounded animal you've
been locked in a room with

and your blood ignites
an insatiable hunger to
be loved.

## SWORD LILY | *Gladiolus hortulanus*

Moments before quietus
the heart races      accelerates
lungs propel a gasp
mouth unrolls the tongue
        holds the weight of my breath
legs convulse
                then suddenly
the bull in charge takes position
        shoves her hooves into steel
                ferociously yells at me
                        "Control it! Control it!"
        I can't.
I scream when I cry.

The body I hold is now a memory
my tears refuse to be complemented
with silence.      I scream

and everyone hears the excavation
of grief packed with fat shoved in
            between bone and muscle

and everyone sees the union
between coral and swords sharpening

Mother?
You see this tongue?

This tongue knows survival
        is not denial of self
                but the strength of a zealous heart

determined to heal.

HYDRANGEA | *Hydrangea macrophylla*

*to Mother*


Your father left me
for dead with soiled pampers
and a scorching lavender blue
larynx on his 1960s green carpet

I laid there limp in the living room

Tears destined to preserve me
I cried for you
I screamed *Mommy*    until I passed out

Craving your presence
cradled me until I was nine

Then at twelve—
I spoke through an eroding esophagus
a belly on fire from secrets
a compressed throat
a murmurous heart

I    told    you    what    happened.

You      did what you could only do
as the frightened abused
little girl   you are

trapped inside an inflated body
of comforting blubber
and sagging  stretched  skin

You were so scared

Your lips shivered

You froze for the next ten years

Yet you have
such a loquacious tongue
when avoiding grief

You tested
my unwavering love
with muteness

You ripped me out
pulled me up
I was once
a dutiful daughter


Now      I am
a bouquet of Hydrangeas
slowly languishing
in the autumn wind
stranded without water

still      I love you
even after you
continued to devour
a pyramid   of marshmallow coated
roasted yams       mash potatoes
cranberries     seasoned stuffing
and slices of baked turkey

when seated sandwiched
between me    and him

Bite after bite
I lost appetite
I began to purge

Your taciturnity
devalued me

Your swollen tongue
nearly broke my dignity

I love you
you tried to protect me—

a woman shielding her daughter
from catcalls and whistles

a woman cursing grown men
on street corners   for staring too long
salivating     desperate to comb
her daughter's twelve-year-old curves

but woman
your silence made you a bystander

I must help you
never stop loving you

You easily feel  unheard
you hyperventilate
your lungs tighten your voice drops
you talk in circles
I remind you to breathe

and although I wish
I could wrest your karma
I can't

Your hair thins
in loneliness

Your blood clots
in worries

I see you
and I forgive you

I hold my truth
regardless   if you hold mine too.

COLUMBINE | *Aquilegia vulgaris*


I.


In the spring
the perennial sorrow
I am the daughter of Columbines


blood and earth
bound together
I yawn my limbs to five corners


Without me
no one would know
the freedom crying gives


a heart not
found on asphalt
but in the steps of me walking away


from machines
from artificial vegetation
from a world of skyscrapers built on wet sand

II.

When I walk
mourning doves hoot

Hawks screech their
caw as they glide above black plumage

Butterflies
flutter to the rhythm of newborn heartbeats

Coyotes
cross the bridge without jumping

Black waters
glisten   entice   ghosts linger

stare at the
bodies determined to jump

the San Fran-
cisco Bay   becomes a puddle

PROTEA | *Protea cynaroides*


The original    flesh
                bone
                blood
                flower boiling from kinship
Source of civilization
    of etiquette
    of elegance
                       families derive from Her spine
                     nations grow from Her womb
She knows    every language
            every intonation
            every pause    given to silence.

Her screams rattle spirits in bodies
Her cries expel the wicked
She spits white phlegm into the fire
She is the Mother who knows
        Her children have been wounded
           households infiltrated.

She    roars
      moves
      emanates life in spite of extinction

She    survives
      thrives
      cradles humanity in Her arms

No one    nothing    can kill Her.

PETUNIA | *Petunia hybrida*


Your silence sharpens the blades of my leaves
      the asymptotic nature of each petal
           the rigidity of my stem in the winter
I stand guilty
enraged in the house of Petunia
         the tobacco not made for smoke
      the resentments of your hissing   comparing   dragging
my name across ripped carpets   burned my knees
      and the furniture with plaque so thick
         I can see the years of negligence.


I carry the knives
      used to slash across your belly
we both hemorrhaged the lost time
stolen childhoods   empty little bodies
         stained with saliva and semen
     unripe braided hair pulled into soil
and to this day   you keep all bedroom doors open.
you always ask me  why   I did not tell you sooner
     I was simply a child in shock
and I keep my door shut.


             Whether blood
comes with me or not


         I heal    I speak.

DANDELION | *Taraxacum erythrospermum*


Come        here lies the girl
            who loved dancing with wind
            blowing wishes on Dandelions
her little hands found hope on a stem. She
hopscotched on cracked pavement pretending
she was in the fields of lush greenery
playing with golden fairies and sparkling pixies
her grieving lungs blew     *one day      life will be better*
but
she froze
stopped breathing
laid awake as long
            as she could
            tasting shards of her father's crack pipe
            five years into his absence.


In the night she was ripped open.
No escape
and no one believed her.
            She died        in nobody's arms.


Today    we find her
            under the debris
                    of collapsed neighborhoods
                            buildings that once housed
                            first-generation children
                            the cooking of tortillas tamales frijoles
            but    are now replaced
                    with white rice and Asian dishes
                    and great white sharks with porcelain white smiles.
I turn her on her side
pat her back as she coughs up the debris. Instantly
our battles to live thaw
            with   the Sun on her fingertips

the stars blown for wishes
the crown of light
          her black frizzled curls mold resembling
the moon of a Dandelion.

MOON FLOWER | *Ipomoea alba*


Moon rises
I open
　　scream
　　　　　remember
and I say

me too

NASTURTIUM | *Tropaeolum tuberosum*


My tongue almost yanked from my mouth
    this body once colonized
        the wind in my leaves almost silenced

I nearly pulled each petal before blossom

I was convinced      my pulse was untrustworthy
           my nectar disdainful
    only worth contemptuousness

but I fought back
    held my breath
        saved my water
                I clenched Earth
            bathed in my own nectar
I knew they would
exhaust themselves    and the pain would stop.

Years later        I screamed

S   T   O   P

PEONY | *Paeonia lactiflora*


Pink

                         ripped

unfolds

                         on my lips

I can barely

                utter the words

living

                      is hard

I can't

breathe.

PROTEA | *Protea compacta*


Behind years of cement
weak walls loud bedrooms
Protea          ruptures open
                stops the erasure of my bliss
                        the body snatching
                                killing of our people
                we scream     *I can't breathe!*
witnesses detained       footage goes viral
        from where       ghosts play checkers with pistols
where

                ancestors used bare hands to kill
where

                the thought *kill yourself* is convincing.
Protea
breathes life
petals of no separation : Africa
                rests near the apex of her stem.
She      extends her arms
         smiles wide

                cowrie shells and purple gums guard
                the children's quest for freedom.
Aposematic skin wards off      bullets   uniforms
                        judges   politicians
                        plea bargains sterilizing the nation.
No resistance    Protea
                transcends
                blossoms in the trenches of struggle
                abolishes slavery.
Ankles untied
        Afro    her halo     each follicle
        a soul   marches to the frontline
                ignites into a crimson funeral pyre.

She    burns    the hands who lost control
                glass pipes and bottles
                doors locked shut with no escape
                the terror once found in my eyes
Protea remains
       unfolds
       dances with the flames chanting
                Black and breathing
                Black and breathing
                Black and breathing.

LOTUS | *Nelumbo nucifera*


I.


They tried to
kill me in silence
pillage the countryside of my body
desecrate the wild.

They tried to
bury me in shallow ponds
tarns to drown cries
near glistening limelight stages.

They tried to
unknowingly    preserve my life
their hands swollen from brandy
cold  wrinkled  greasy ignited light from soil.

My roots    now
strengthened    my bones in formation
I emerge slowly uprising in the night.  I rise
in the glimmer of untamable waters

I live.

II.

and I watched her
renounce turbid lies billboards of deceit.

I watched her
purify ruptured vessels of her spirit.

She thought she was supposed to die
yet I watched her live

risk everything to learn love
trust an unfamiliar embrace from clean hands.

Fresh waters through the curvature of her stem
she grew ascending healing releasing

an oscillating upsurge of surrender
arms unfold thighs widen.

She breathes above sunlit waters and dances
dances wildly    she is within me.

## LAVENDER | *Lavandula angustifolia*

Lavender stands on her feet
stares wide-eyed into the camera
no smile    just curls    and those eyes
living on the corner    spread out across dirt
by empty towns          near front lawns
by abandoned cars    in stolen bedrooms
around the block from failed brick
        schoolkid penitentiaries
down the street from lost prayers
and serious in-demand frivolous portraits.

She tells me    once-kept secrets
her frayed skin softens under the sun
she deepens my breath    loosens tense muscles
complements the faith of early autumn
arms crumple tired coats
the lifespan of armor    dies too with the soldier
roots prepare for a lock-in    drones patrol the skies
the purest smile penetrates the bulletproof
bees    remain devout all year long
        fly through thickened air
        swarm home escaping the flames.
They return only to rest with Lavender
The aroma    softens their sting
and protects her    from the roaming mice    old farmers'
hands    hungry to trespass    her skin again.
"No more" she says    as she guards
young flowers rising.

She    is the grin of twilight.

LILAC | *Syringa vulgaris*
*to Grandfather*


Take your filthy hands off me.


I SAID— Take your scarred wounded
hands    off me.

Your weight has no
power over
my wobbly toddler knees.

Your old construction hands    calloused
with generations of incest
beatings children screaming pulverized
these amethyst flowers.

I remember choking on the size
of your retired labor-union
tongue when my gums were getting ready
to release their first set of baby teeth.

I remember you stretching my legs
after kindergarten graduation
I stopped liking school then my tights stained
a rite of passage to the first grade.

I remember you spreading my legs
at night when Grandma went to take a
       l     o     n    g
bath. Your oldest son pulled the same move
like father like son two years later.
        His gallant badge radiated from
                extinguishing fires     your son
                    this firefighter used his hands to
      burn the lips between my thighs     yet I

survived. A field of Lilacs who
run with the four directions
Great Spirit oversees this field. I

clear out my throat
each time I taste your mucoid saliva. I

lose my appetite          when  I feel
your fingers circling my soft areolas. I

smudge my body          with sage sweetgrass rose petals
          transmuting your residual sweat
                    into tears leading me to the Ocean.

I scream into waves.
Yemaya holds me          the shore
line's salty foam releases my prayers.

I dive deep soar high
I unwind on the spine of a humpback whale.

Her oscillating muffled words travel miles.
Her cryptic tones swirl violet within my aura.


I DECLARE—
you
have NO
POWER over me!
                    You have NO POWER
                    over
                    me!
                              YOU
                              HAVE
                              NO
                              POWER
                              OVER
                              ME!

When dawn breaks     I rise
in the direction
of the East     I pick
up shovel and seeds

                I sow     I weep
          I sow I weep I sow I weep
      for many moons I renew
an ethereal field of Lilacs!


Swallowtail butterflies rest
      on petals pulsating purpureal shades
        leaves dance while oak trees wave their arms
in celebration. At last

I return to where I first saw her
where I first see me as a little girl

and where I tell her
I love you

I've always loved you
and I never left you

I never will leave you.
She roams in this field.


She     Rests     In     Power.

# ANNUAL

## DAHLIA | *Dahlia pinnata*

In the red desert
of burnt flesh and snake skeletons

I flower
in wavering contemplation

swirl in caskets of unfed generals    vultures
circumnavigate above      begrudgingly

I remain graceful with an eagle's stare
stand and reveal an eagle's wingspan

I tower the shrubs below me
and laugh at quarrels mice have with themselves

yet when memories
break the dams of my eyes

I no longer bear
witness to life      smoke soils the sky

body remains still
yet I am nowhere to be found.

CHRYSANTHEMUM | *Chrysanthemum morifolium*


and  she pours
breaks the sky     with tears
cracks windchimes with her teeth
She beats      on  my front door
feeble walls          rooftops
windowsills
tremble            I am left shaking
entangled
        in the violaceous
                clusters of her hair
my body at night
alone    freezes      one eye
remains open when asleep
stomach habitually stressed     tight
hurts to digest and release    legs stiff
knees crack     heart palpitates
ears easily hear  a cough through walls
cries through buildings
            yet        when moon
                    rises
I bathe in
her light :  the high tides
            the reverence
            the petrichor
            the reassurance
            the hope : one day
this body
will know

Love.

## MORNING GLORY | *Ipomoea purpurea*


I rest on the grave of who
stood defeated
dress stained      wrinkled
cold in mildew
        like *his* hands
                her body    an acquisition.
With sewn lips heavy eyelids
she hid behind
fantasies
of a white savior
        coming to rescue her
                (but no one ever came).


So for years    she grew      staggered
        to the nearest couch    barstool
        she never did
                celebrate
                the rise and set
                        of sun and moon.


May she rest in power      have
a childhood in peace          as I walk
        this path
        climb this old trellis
        be the purple pressed
        into stars      incubating
                the piercing opalescent light
                        within her.


Vines tenaciously latch on-
to ligneous fences

each stride I take       must be done
in patience.


She is within me    as I ascend
up the meandering
rivers of my legs
I am Morning Glory.


Balance assembles freedom
I awake with sun
I renew my vow to life.

MARIGOLD | *Tagetes erecta*


Eyes of the sun      stare outside a bus window
a crackhead father dangles cheap rocks in one hand
and clenches a disposable lighter      (the only fire he feels)
in another.

Marigold      with torn ruffles extends her arms
stretches her fingers
she emanates sacral rays of a brazen orange and yellow
for the lost      resistant      spirits who only recognize her
in darkness.

They see their lantern      through timeless fog
cigarette smoke      shots of tequila.  Marigold sees her
father.      His spirit floats
but the orange sun still loves him      tries to guide his spirit
to the light

the crack vanishes      but he refuses to rest by his altar.
Marigold now sees her mother      a single mother
wobbling down dirty city streets      past forgotten altars
sacrificing last pennies on Catholic uniforms

back and knees sore from carrying groceries
ruptured relationships      a hernia from carrying a stroller
up three flights of stairs      each day      for another fatherless
baby.      Stubborn blood stands against chimes
warbling on wintry windy nights.

She is the wild bull inflamed      who does not bleed.
Her weight marks her endurance : a path she cleaved ::
her fat and hair mark her protection      when she fights
she fights to kill.
She      is the one alive      who reminds Marigold—

everything can be healed.

EUCALYPTUS | *Eucalyptus globulus*
*to Aunt Gina*


I.


You     were among the first
        to ever hold me
        witness my smiling gums.

I was safe in your arms
        unaware of
        how    unsafe   I was
in the walls you held me in.

You     cradled me as if
        *you* were my mother
        and for years     I did not
see the slit on your wrist.

You disappeared often
        an enigma    born
        in the winter   a new
born-again    Pentecostal Christian
        glamorous fashion
                controlled disposition
Grandmother    loved you    the most.

When news of your cancer
        welcomed me back from
        D.C.  I stood by
the door shocked.

Your expiration date
        ripped my duffle bag

open.

II.

The last familial holiday
was Mother's Day. We saw you
dressed in the black underlining your
paleness   body swelling.   No one
spoke of cancer    of dying   of
how to prepare for your absence
in the upcoming years of our lives.

No—     we grieve in silence
confront truth      (never)
or only when alone

(family tradition).

III.

Two months later     I walk in
on the last Monday of your life.
Bundles of burgundy Eucalyptus
greeted me on the front porch.

Each leaf reminded me of
the mildly sweet aroma
death sometimes has.

Each leaf initiated
the resolution of congestive
ancestral brokenness.

The closer I reached for the door
the closer I smelled death of a woman.

When I saw you    I saw what was left
of your body    swollen even more
with swarming armies
of cannibalistic cells    secretive tumors
we had no choice but to surrender to.

                Spirit was counting down
             your last breath
         a victory preparing for loss.

*What have you learned in this lifetime?*
I asked
relying on oxygen tubes
you spoke—

*When I look into the abyss of my own vanity*
*I can no longer look at the struggles of others*
*in condescending superiority.*

                              I heard Christ
                          wrote each word down
                      then left.

By Friday afternoon
you were nowhere
to be found.

ANGEL'S TRUMPET | *Brugmansia*


and I am here      dangling
from screams buried in dirt

this family      this country
wears hypocrisy      like a hagfish

or lamprey      found in Saks Fifth Avenue fur
the parasite appears rich

from scraps of skin and hair
twirls in blood of children's fingers

stitching line by line
they will one day die      a premature death

Artificial Light and Intelligence
cannot conceal core cavities

found in the body
found in dead tree trunks

found in unraveling roots   conduct
policies      corporations      this nation's

constitution      law is nothing
but a series of loopholes

a game of chess
wear your polo sweater

the canon condones torture genocide rape
the telling of we were never equal

I am the Angel's Trumpet
you touch me long enough

chew on my petals  swallow me whole
and I kill you      step back      listen

to the voices near street corners
backyards front lawns

rows of houses      mom-and-pop
shops apartment complexes

where there is land
there is blood

and I play you the dead   deprived   devalued
left to lie in pools of blood

and their blood seeps into my soil
from bodies   killed   stolen

I transmute the shock to love!

CHAMOMILE | *Matricaria chamomilla*


I ran through a storm once that lasted ten years
the rain drenched my clothes
my face streaked with cheap eyeliner

no one could tell how old my tears were
until I found the sliver of dirt between concrete
and the illumination of

a once-retired smile
a hopeless squint of plucked feathers
a vinyl box of thank-you cards

the wind blew and guided me
I ignored its warning    at times
saw light through shattered windshields

and I mastered the art of shattering.
To mourn the existence of waiting
in line to die

is to    tolerate my own breath
          stomach the laments
          face life calmly

and slowly blossom    to a kettle boiling.

RAIN LILY | *Zephyranthes grandiflora*


One day you'll read the lines on my face
know the lawlessness under my skin    in my bones

and you'll know the silence each crevice holds
from the black of my blood to the plaque behind molars

the scars of finding gold. You'll see me shine
like a glass case of knives

and you'll know the sharpness of each tooth
how children speak with knotted tongues

how men in power lost control of their hands
how bystanders became politicians.

I tore skin    ran across the plains
sought the Pacific rested near redwoods

I am the flowers of west wind.

## AMARANTH | *Amaranthus*


Remember this seed
impervious to roundup   bleach   vinegar
was buried alone   in the Spring
along the northern Californian coast
near trails of used crack pipes
homicidal hands   suppressed laments.


New blood   simmered   under the sun
I grew   listening to my mother   in tears
and her occasional laughs on the barstool
proud   that for the first time
life   lived   inside   her.


Every day I laid in fetal position
listening to the growing formation of my bones
each organ learning to function
a throbbing heart in anguish.


I knew   one day
petals will be contorted
stained by old men
stem and pistil   desecrated.
I will one day have
the choice: fight   or   surrender
to transcend!


A germinating resentment
to live   die   grew inside my veins.
I felt captive in my mother's womb
I had to escape! She screamed
in agony   swore she
was dying   requested her last rites
from a priest Sunday morning
and nuns   nurses   witnesses
rose as   I   arrived   premature

impatient    a secret.

I immediately demanded
to renegotiate my vow to life.
My screams reverberated across a sterile room
eventually I sprouted
in the darkness of shadows    I swayed.

Pacific winds coddled me reminding me
to feel stay humbled wait
renounce all desires to control.

Liberty is not given
lies in the source the roots the route
of my existence.

After soil and sun slowly began draining
my imperiousness    I died
an unknown dictator was reborn a slave

and died again   the irradiance
rinses my veins
revitalizes each petal.

Today    I    live    wild!

GAZANIA | *Gazania linearis*


I    alone    extinguish
that raptorial yearning
to taste butter on tongue
rub honey       between fingers

tangerine lips pucker
up for a kiss    when planted
in full sun       when dresses
silhouette the galaxy

of my body among
sequined stars rhinestone laughter
I open          when planted
in full sun          flow of Oshun

I exceed the price of
elephant tusk    fresh waters
bow        continents offer
ripe oranges    and cinnamon

to boil the bones of
who stole my mother's body.

AZALEA | *Rhododendron*


Do not underestimate my power
I am woman

the divine feminine
My time is now

I barricade the drilled wells
once punctured into my womb

I excavate each hook oil pipeline
once pierced inside me

My skin the cerise my body these petals
cannot be stretched any further by despotic hands

My water is sacred  my love is pure
despite contamination and abuse

I fought to live
now live to thrive

Do not underestimate my power
I am woman

FUCHSIA | *Fuchsia magellanica*


Believe me.

My cracked lips and stained tongue
a burning stomach in a no-backbone bedroom
did not deter      the swift flight of endurance
the remembrance of sweetness  of survival.

Hummingbirds came once I tasted my
tears     yet sometimes I still close my eyes
to the Sun.    I see the glaring red
of my florid skin        swollen inside
irritated infected from
pesticides        the warmth of invasion
                of his cold fingers inside.

I cry     growl     slice arteries with teeth.
I wrestle with the treachery of  men  until
I          twirl prayers into beads of nectar
           break the hex of hatred
           ground the betrayal into fertile land.

I grow from the whispers
of *ssshhhh . . . don't tell no body.*    Fingers over lips
today my mouth like legs rests wide
open.

Believe me.
He knew someone would.

GLOSSARY | *Glossarium*

**A — Annual: grown year-round**
**P — Perennial: seasonally grown**

AMARANTH | *Amaranthus* **(A/P)**
Native to North and South America • immortality

ANGEL'S TRUMPET | *Brugmansia* **(A/P)**
Native to South America • transformative • expanding consciousness/
awareness • infamous for its deadly toxicity and hallucinogenic
properties

AZALEA | *Rhododendron* **(A)**
Native to Asia, Europe, and North America • femininity • womanhood
• self-care

BLEEDING HEART | *Lamprocapnos spectabilis* **(P)**
Native to Asia • rejected love • releasing emotions • sensitivity

CAROLINA LUPINE | *Thermopsis villosa* **(P)**
Native to North America • awareness • happiness • gentleness

CHAMOMILE | *Matricaria chamomilla* **(A/P)**
Native to Europe • "energy in adversity" • release of tension in mind and body

CHERRY PLUM | *Prunus cerasifera* **(P)**
Native to Asia, Europe, and North America • releasing the fear of losing control and causing harm to others

CHRYSANTHEMUM | *Chrysanthemum morifolium* **(A/P)**
Native to Asia and Europe • loyalty • devotion • recovery • support

CLEMATIS | *Clematis virginiana* **(P)**
Native to North America • ingenuity • artifice • mental prowess

COLUMBINE | *Aquilegia vulgaris* **(P)**
Native to Europe • self-love • strength • wisdom

CROCUS | *Crocus sativus* **(P)**
Native to Asia • truth • dignity • pride • joy

DAHLIA | *Dahlia pinnata* **(A)**
Native to North America (Mexico's national flower) • inner strength • power • staying focused

DANDELION | *Taraxacum erythrospermum* **(P)**
Native to North America • survival • healing • long lasting joy

EUCALYPTUS | *Eucalyptus globulus* **(A/P)**
Native to Australia • "the holy tree of aboriginals" • protection • purity • division between heaven and earth

EVENING PRIMROSE | *Oenothera biennis* **(P)**
Native to North America • eternal love • beauty

FUCHSIA | *Fuchsia magellanica* **(A/P)**
Native to South America • confiding love

GARDENIA | *Gardenia jasminoides* **(P)**
Native to Africa, Asia, and Pacific Islands • trust • purity • renewal • protection

GAZANIA | *Gazania linearis* **(A)**
Native to Africa • "the butter flower" • wealth and richness

HIBISCUS | *Hibiscus rosa-sinensis* **(P)**
Native to Asia • femininity • fleeting beauty/love

HYDRANGEA | *Hydrangea macrophylla* (P)
Native to Japan • heartfelt honesty • deeper understanding • abundance
• prosperity

INDIGO | *Baptisia australis* **(P)**
Native to North America • mystery • intuition • wisdom • justice

IRIS | *Iris germanica* **(P)**
Native to Europe • wisdom • valor

LAVENDER | *Lavandula angustifolia* **(P)**
Native to the Mediterranean • purity • devotion • grace • serenity

LILAC | *Syringa vulgaris* **(P)**
Native to Europe and North America • innocence • love • transcendence

LOTUS | *Nelumbo nucifera* **(P)**
Native to Africa and Asia • enlightenment • purity • the triumph over
trauma • patience

MAGNOLIA | *Magnolia grandiflora* **(P)**
Native to North America • dignity • purity • femininity

MARIGOLD | *Tagetes erecta* **(A/P)**
Native to South America • "herb of the sun" • despair and grief •
celebrating the dead • promoting good relations

MOON FLOWER | *Ipomoea alba* **(P)**
Native to North America • "blossoming in dark times" • confronting the
shadow of self

MORNING GLORY | *Ipomoea purpurea* **(A/P)**
Native to North and Central America • mortality • unrequited love

NASTURTIUM | *Tropaeolum tuberosum* **(P)**
Native to South America • conquest • strong in combat

NOPAL CACTUS | *Opuntia macrocentra* **(P)**
Native to North and South America • protection • chastity • resilient

ORCHID | *Orchidaceae phalaenopsis* **(P)**
Native to Asia and Pacific Islands • strength • beauty • love

PEONY | *Paeonia lactiflora* **(P)**
Native to Asia • honor • compassion • wealth

PETUNIA | *Petunia hybrida* **(P)**
Native to South America • anger • resentment • desire for peace

PROTEA | *Protea compacta* **(P)**
Native to Africa • transformation • courage

PROTEA | *Protea cynaroides* **(P)**
Native to Africa • diversity • change

RAIN LILY | *Zephyranthes grandiflora* **(A/P)**
Native to Central and South America • loss • innocence restored after death

SEASIDE DAISY | *Erigeron glaucus* **(P)**
Native to North America • purity

SWORD LILY | *Gladiolus hortulanus* **(P)**
Native to Africa, Asia, and Mediterranean Europe • strength • faith • never give up

SOURCES

flowermeaning.com • flowerinfo.org • ftd.com • theflowerexpert.com • bachflower.com • wikipedia.com

## ACKNOWLEDGEMENTS | *Additae*

First and foremost, I thank the undeniable force in my life, a power greater than me—my Creator, the Great Spirit. With you, all is possible. I am restored and filled with hope, gratitude, and joy.

I thank all of my family. Blood no blood—you are my bedrock. You show me how to live, fight for my joy, and let live one day at a time. With you, we can heal. I love you.

I thank June Jordan, her poetry, her legacy, and her bringing the Poetry for the People program to UC Berkeley. I thank Aya de Leon for her leadership and her devotion to Poetry for the People. Your wisdom, your words, your strength, and your nurture gave me the soil to conceive this book.

I thank the Poetician for reading my earliest drafts of poems contained in this collection. Your love, patience, and mentorship was the water to have this book sprout. I love you.

I thank all the curators, poets, and literary patrons I have met, read with, and listened to, especially those in the San Francisco Bay Area. I have been inspired by you countless times and I thank you all for listening and engaging with the drafts of these poems contained in this book.

I thank the editors of the following journals, small presses, and online platforms for publishing early versions of poems contained in this book: *Atlanta Review, Snapdragon: A Journal of Art & Healing, For Women Who Roar* magazine, *Mookychick, Rag Queen Periodical, For Harriet's Soar, Digging Through the Fat* (Digging Press), *Tilde - A Literary Journal* (Thirty West Publishing House), *GIANTHOLOGY*, and Dream Pop Press.

I thank the editors of anthologies *Love With Accountability: Digging Up the Roots of Child Sexual Abuse* (AK Press, 2019) and *Still Here San Francisco* (Foglifter Press, 2019). Aishah, my comrade, my fellow survivor, you are my exemplar of resiliency. You continuously teach me what activism, survivorship visibility, art, and love can do to transform society. I appreciate you. Natalia and Mason, I see you. I appreciate you. We OUT here! 4-1-5. San Francisco. Thank you for being among the ones preserving the arteries of the city.

Lastly and most sincerely, I deeply thank Jennifer Lewis and Jessie Carver—Red Light Lit Press. As a curated multimedia series, RLL is a strong pillar for community. As a press, y'all are monumental for innovative breakthroughs. I see you. I appreciate you. So much. Thank you for believing in the work. Thank you for your love, your patience, your dedication, your transparency, your brilliance, your magic.

Thank you.

Thank you.

Thank you.

## About Red Light Lit

Red Light Lit is devoted to writers, artists, and musicians who explore love, relationships, sexuality, identity, and gender. Since our founding in 2013, we have published 10 literary journals and produced over 100 live shows (including in Austin, Chicago, Los Angeles, Portland, San Francisco, and Seattle). In 2019, Red Light Lit published the poetry anthology *Love Is the Drug & Other Dark Poems*; and in 2020, it published *Unearth [The Flowers]* by Thea Matthews, its first single-author poetry collection.

www.redlightlit.com
@redlightlit

CPSIA information can be obtained
at www.ICGtesting.com
Printed in the USA
FSHW011919250220
67527FS